14 Years I

Eve MacFarlane

14 Years Later

For Sam & Sean

Eve MacFarlane

14 Years Later

Contents

Introduction

15th April 2007

Lorna Jane

Childhood

Dad

Mental Health

Outro

Eve MacFarlane

14 Years Later

Introduction

Having just turned eighteen, I thought this year would be the best time to write this book. It's something I've wanted to do for a while. The past fourteen years of my life have been very different to what was once expected. It took a dramatic turn and created drastic changes for my family.

I'm not so clear on how to begin a story like this as it is a very complicated and long one with a variety of experiences. There are so many different aspects and dimensions of what losing a parent at such a young age creates. This event has been the biggest thing to impact and shape my life and this experience of mine is always something I have grown up continuously thinking about and questioning. It's hard to rationalise something that doesn't truly have a valid reason which as a result makes it hard to find any closure. I want to share my experiences and explain the realities of growing up without a mother. I hope this book brings understanding to my Dad and the people who have been involved in my life and have always wanted to help. I want to encourage people through reading this book to develop an open-minded and considerate mindset. Long term effects of many things in life aren't always clear and apparent and sometimes it is necessary to consider this. Lots of people are fighting some sort of battle that you may not know about and a little bit of support can really go a long way. My support system over the years has been so incredible and I am eternally grateful.

I've learnt a lot throughout my upbringing. A lot about people, mental health, expectations, life. Calculating the path without a mother figure will always be one of the hardest things I've ever done but I'm eighteen now and I have successfully made it to adult-hood. This life was never predicted to be this way for me and my brothers but it has become more natural and easier to deal with over the years. Losing a mother at a young age can affect your personality and upbringing as essentially you've lost 50% of your guidance. It's not easy to find that guidance anywhere else. There is nothing to replace it. Everything becomes a bit unbalanced. You can work with it and find ways to make it easier but nothing will truly make up for what's lost. You just learn the different ways to deal with it and formulate your own navigation through it all. In the end, it is manageable and I hope this book shows you the truth of that.

This is my story about growing up without a mother.

14 Years Later

Eve MacFarlane

14 Years Later

15th April 2007

On Sunday the 15th of April 2007, my mother, Lorna Jane MacFarlane, passed away from sudden heart failure.

My Mum was taken into hospital in the evening of the 14th of April due to an unexplainable seizure and held there unconscious overnight. She passed away at ten minutes to ten in the morning of the 15th surrounded by the people closest to her.

This day was extremely confusing to me. It's all a bit blurry and I don't remember the reality really sinking in. I had no idea what was going on and why my house was filled with people whose faces were flooded with tears. Recently, I have been informed of several experiences of this day from different people and understood the routine of the day from many different perspectives.

At four years old, life is always so simple and so carefree. You are most definitely not prepared to accept and understand life changing news like this. I didn't have the capability to comprehend or process my Mum's death. To me, I'm pretty sure this day just consisted of seeing lots of friends and family. I had no other thoughts. Of course, I would have been told the news but I wouldn't have understood it. In some ways, this may have been better as all of the feelings came gradually to me over time. It was never sudden in my head and I never felt the instant shock. I think I remember snippets from the day like being carried around and hugged a lot but I've never been sure if I created those images in my head from what people have said or if I really do remember them.

I've been told that on this day, I was so confused and very clueless to the reality of it all. I couldn't understand why everyone was crying. It wasn't a normal sight for me. Usually, I was the one crying. When you see adults cry at such a young age it confuses you as you think crying is only something that children do. Lots of parents hide their hurt from their children which is normal. Children wouldn't be able to give you the support you need when they rely on you so much. So I think being surrounded by distressed adults was where my confusion started.

14 Years Later

My Dad and some other adults took me and my brothers to the park in the afternoon. When I picture that, I see three young children playing on the swings carefree with no idea of the sudden change of their life and the impact this event will have on their lives. When I was told this, it made it all feel real for a second. It puts it into a clearer perspective. Being told about the life I lived with my Mum or just soon after she passed away makes it feel like much more of a real thing because I have nothing to really base what life was like back then off. My memories of it all are too vague and pretty much non-existent. Hearing new things about this time of my life always makes it feel more like I was actually there, mentally there. I don't remember my life before my Mum passed. I think her death marked the beginning of where my proper memories started because this event was so prominent and such a big deal that maybe it made me start to feel things. This time of my life is very hard to recollect so being told about the memories from this day, like going to the park, just feels like a story from the distant past that I was never present for. It just feels like I wasn't really living through the time of it all happening. I guess being so young, your feelings aren't so apparent and you don't think too much about things, let alone have the capability to rationalise them.

Eve MacFarlane

My Dad came back from the hospital and got me and my brothers together to tell us what was going on. Once I was told the news, apparently I was a bit all over the place. I was wandering in and out of the house questioning why my Dad and brothers were crying. It was inevitable that I wouldn't have understood at that age. Being at ages four, six and nine, me and my brothers all processed it differently, if at all. My eldest brother knew my Mum the best which made how he dealt with it different to me and my other brother, not better, not worse, just different.

The reality and realisation of my Mum's passing became more apparent and easier to understand with the ongoing years. However, this day does still haunt me. It haunts me through imagining the pain and shock people felt. It's never something I will be able to comprehend. It always breaks my heart thinking about it and it forever will. I never had to deal with that sudden gut-wrenching heart drop feeling like everybody else.

I think about my Dad and the shock and fear he must have felt. The double feeling of losing someone close to you and losing your children's mother. How do you prepare yourself to raise three young children on your own while working a full time job? How do you prepare yourself to act as a mother and a father at the same time? How do you instantly change pretty much everything

14 Years Later

about your current lifestyle? How do you grieve when there is so much responsibility? How do you carry on? My Dad always said to me in response to these questions; 'you just have to'. But he didn't have to. He could have given up. So easily. He could have moved away, started a new life, left the past behind, forgotten everything. But he didn't. He stayed.

My Mum's passing had such an impact. My aunties and uncle lost their little sister, my Nana and Papa lost their daughter, cousins lost a cousin, nieces and nephews lost an auntie, friends lost a friend, potentially some of the closest people to her in her life. I don't know what goes through someone's mind when something like this happens.

For so long, my Mum was the only death close to me that I'd ever experienced, but then again, I don't feel like I fully really did experience her death, I experienced her loss. But what did go through all of these people's minds? I honestly couldn't tell you what went through my mind. Nothing. I had no feeling. Not in a numb sense, just in an extremely naive sense. My age really saved me from potentially one of the darkest places I could ever have been in. What I'm saying is that I believe there are two types of pain in this situation. The instant shock gut wrenching feeling and then the grieving. My age saved the gut wrenching feeling. I say

15

this to help further portray the lack of presence and existence I felt in my own Mum's life. My grieving is different. I feel it every single day of my life and I won't ever get over it. It's like there's just an empty void clinging to me wherever I go and it won't ever heal.

When I was a young teenager, I looked through a box of everything regarding her funeral. I saw all of the cards. I saw the sign-ins of the people who attended the funeral. Everyone was there. Even my teachers were there. It was so strange for me to read all of the cards from such a significant time of my life that I felt like I didn't even live through. My mother was a stranger to me. This event was probably the biggest moment of my life but I didn't even feel present. There were messages on the cards like 'call me if you need someone to look after the kids' and people leaving their addresses and phone numbers. This is another thing that made it all feel real again. It puts me into a little daze of feeling present in it all for a couple of seconds. Like this isn't a story. It really happened. It makes me think of the feelings my Dad must have had and how he must have felt reading all of the cards. Numb probably. It must have been hard to take in any information. It would be hard to take in anything for weeks, months even, after a traumatic event like that happens. I just can't get over that, ever.

14 Years Later

Everyone would have known it wasn't going to be easy. I can imagine them writing the cards. Some people signed it with 'I have no words, just God bless you all'. People knew it wasn't normal. They knew how much of an impact it would have for our future. My Mum's death isn't something that just happens in life. It was such an out-of-nowhere unexplainable occurrence. Nobody expected it and this is why I cannot for the life of me, begin to even understand why it just had to be this way. Every day of my life, I am stuck hopelessly searching for the answer to my question 'why?'

It's hard to explain this day of my life. Sometimes, I don't really feel like it's my experience to tell. I didn't feel the way other people felt. I didn't feel the trauma nor do I feel any PTSD from this day. I was pretty fine really. It's too much of a blur to me to thoroughly understand or remember the happenings of the day. I can only go off what I've been told. I feel it through other people. Especially my Dad.

Being the youngest in my family at this time meant that I spent the least time with my Mum. Even though my oldest brother was nine, there were still so many things he hadn't experienced yet and so much that he couldn't understand. He knew my Mum was no longer with us but how do you know where she is? I was told my brothers never really spoke about it or asked about it growing up. However, we have discussed it a lot over recent years. There's just always a limit to what there is to say. There becomes a limit on the stories you can tell about someone who is no longer here to create any more. We were all so young and we all felt it so differently. It affected us in such different ways that just because we all lost someone of the same title to each other, it was still such a different loss.

I want to know how everybody else experienced life with her, what she meant to them, how much she meant to them. But I wish I knew it all myself. Why do I have to ask people any time I ever want to know anything about my Mum? She is such a huge part of me but such a stranger.

Every 15th of April feels weird to me. Every year. I say weird because it's a significant life changing date of mine but not one that I recall having a feeling for. I know for some people this date could bring back traumatising unwanted feelings. Similar to what they'd felt in 2007. I guess I don't really know how to feel on this day. It's been fourteen years now, it's easier. People aren't grieving in the same ways they used to be. It's not as raw and fresh anymore. But that adds to the sadness. Grieving has an expiry date. It gets to a point where you can't take any more time off or time out as it becomes unhealthy or in some ways, irrational. I don't feel like I

14 Years Later

had a specific grieving time or any real closure. I wouldn't have understood a funeral at that age even if I had been there. So it comes to me in doses everytime I see, hear or feel something that reminds me of the realities of now. Like minutes or seconds to grieve. I just feel like it's too late for closure now. Things fade. The fourteenth year is never considered to be as sad as the first, second or third but I didn't understand how to grieve back then.

It's also become apparent to me that to the people who only knew me after my Mum died, it's all referred to as 'my Mum passed away when I was young' or 'Eve's Mum died when she was young'. To the people who were around at the time, it's referred to as 'my Mum's death' or 'Lorna's death' because it was a significant event they lived through and felt the effects of not just a story they've heard. I lived through it as well but to me it's never not been a story. This is just another way of explaining the distance I feel to it all. What I mean is that, to the people I've met over the recent years, the connection or link to my Mum is through me or my family. Almost like she didn't really ever exist throughout their lifetime. This is why she feels like a stranger to me. And most of the connections I have to her through other people are my family that we don't live close enough to, to go and see everyday. I guess what I'm saying is that I find it hard to feel close to my Mum.

I also took some time recently to speak to family and friends about this day and what it was like to them. These conversations really hit me because it was a new explanation other than from my Dad about the dramatics of the day and all of the feelings involved. My Uncle told me, every day for years after, he didn't wake up not thinking about my Mum. It's strange to me because it's such a different feeling to what I've had over the years. From a completely different perspective. It was such a disastrous and unexpected day that really would haunt anyone close to my Mum but hearing first hand the routine of the day and the effects it had on people close to her was really hard to hear. Her friends told me who she was, what she talked about, how she acted, what she liked, who she was.

Everyone in life has different experiences, perceptions and relationships with each other and so hearing all of the different stories people have about my Mum from so many angles has been so interesting. It just furthers the point that she really did live an important and real life, even though I was never there to see it all.

During the time of my Mum's death, one of the closest people to her would have probably been her boyfriend.

14 Years Later

My Mum and Dad were separated and were both in different relationships when she passed. Recently, I spoke to my Mum's boyfriend at the time. This was a big deal to me as I hadn't spoken to or seen him for over ten years. I remember his house and staying with him for weekends with my brothers but my recollection of how he looked and sounded was none. Over the years, I'd built up an image of him based on the period of my life that I knew him. He had a daughter who we spent a lot of time with and whom I've sometimes been in contact with over the years briefly on social media. Anyway, I spoke to this man and he was so lovely. This was a completely new perspective to consider. He lost his girlfriend. He must have been so heartbroken. And there was literally nothing he could do about it. It's like you're just forced to forget and move on because you're now all alone. My family all had each other to grieve with and heal with but as much as he was close with my family, he must have felt very alone in some way. Speaking to him really opened my eyes to his type of feeling and hurt. He told me another side of who she was and what she was like. I think it really hit him hard and he also found it extremely incomprehensible. She was living a normal life, in contact with him every single day and it's like she just disappeared into thin air. Life doesn't just go back to normal. There is now a huge hole that you can't fill. How do you just adjust back to normal life? It still blows my mind how something like this can happen. In times like this, it must feel so isolating. The people you see in town or where you live, completely oblivious to the news that has just crushed your world and they go about their lives like nothing has changed. Because nothing has changed for them. The world doesn't stop turning. You just have to adjust to it. No matter how numb you are. Part of relationships in life are supporting each other and being there for each other to confide in, but how do you confide in someone who isn't here anymore, about someone who isn't here anymore? How do you stop subconsciously waiting for them to come home realising that they never will? Who do you now talk to about your day? How lonely.

14 Years Later

Lorna Jane

Lorna Jane. Who was she? What did she mean to people? Who was she to me? Let me tell you.

My Mum was one of five siblings. She had three sisters and one brother. She was born on the 22nd July 1964 in Edinburgh and raised in Selkirk. She had her first child in 1998, her second in 2001 and her third, me, in 2003. Throughout her later life, she lived in Berkshire, Dublin, Bristol, Rossett and Wrexham and travelled abroad to many places like Mallorca, Menorca, Marbella, Rhodes, Corfu and Prague.

She is described as easy-going, beautiful, hard-working and considerate. I was always told that she thought the world of my brothers and me and was always praising us and showing so much love towards us. From speaking to several people, I have discovered that she was quite compassionate and understood other people's pain. She also had a huge heart and had so much time for everybody. She really valued her friends and loved being a Mum.

I have no memories of my Mum. I don't know what she sounded like, how she acted, how she spoke, how she laughed. I have no recollection of any of it. Sometimes I wonder, if I didn't see pictures of her, would I really know what she looked like? It wasn't common before 2007 for people to constantly record everything and for there to be countless videos with sound to listen to so I don't have much material to be able to form a detailed image of her from.

I say I miss my Mum and I do but I'm not exactly sure what I miss as I never truly knew her and who she was. There's only so much someone can tell you about someone. It's not the same. It never will be. You can only really gauge what someone is like by speaking to them yourself and spending long amounts of time consistently with them. It's been hard for me to accept that I never knew my Mum. For eternity, every person that I will ever speak to about my Mum will have known her better than or the same as me. I don't even need to know her better than anyone, I just want to know her full stop. I still to this day find it baffling that there's just such a gap. I know the food she liked, the places she

14 Years Later

went, the people she spoke to but I never knew, her. My Dad has spent time over the years talking to me about her life and who she was but it could never be anything that I could gather a picture from or remember. There are no events that he could talk about with me and my Mum both there that I'd recall. I've seen photos of me with my Mum but it's like a different person with her. Like she's holding this child that just isn't really me. I have no recollection of any of the photos being taken or the moments leading up to it. I just feel a huge distance from my Mum.

My age really protected me. I didn't have the mental ability to feel properly. Family, friends and teachers would have been so aware of the impact my Mum's death would have had for the future of me and my brothers but we ourselves, were just so naive, which I guess was for the better. I had no idea what was happening. It's an era of my life that is so extremely hard for me to understand that I have no idea where to even begin when considering what everything felt like and all of the changes that instantly happened.

When somebody passes away, everything becomes limited. You run out of photos, out of memories, out of stories. There is no longer the ability to create more of everything. All I know and learn about my Mum is what people tell me but what happens when there's nothing left to tell?

I feel so disappointed and gutted that I never knew my Mum. It's all just been stolen from me. For so many years, I've longed for a connection to my Mum or just something to hold on to but I can never find anything. She just feels so severely distant to me. It's such a huge part of my life that's just stripped away instantly with no explanation. I didn't get the chance to feel anything. I don't know what it's like to live life with a Mum. It will never make sense to me. There's so much truth in not knowing what you've got until it's gone. If I knew my Mum wasn't going to make it through to another day, I would have held onto her so tightly but there was just absolutely no warning whatsoever.

It can sometimes affect me when I notice people taking their mothers for granted and not being appreciative but it just forms from not coming to terms with the value. You could say that about anyone though. You don't just predict that your Mum, Dad, brother, sister, auntie, uncle or friend could pass away suddenly with no cause. I'm guilty of not fully appreciating people as well. It's quite a subconscious thing as well so it's not something I'd hold against anyone. But I just hope this could be a message to appreciate what you have. For me as well, I have so much to appreciate too.

14 Years Later

In recent years, when significant events in my life happened, like my sixteenth and eighteenth birthday, it really made me think about my Mum. I wanted her to be there. Why couldn't she see her daughter turn eighteen? Why can't I celebrate her birthday every year with her? I want her to meet my friends. I want her to see the things I've done and the places I've been. I want to take her there. I want to take her to my favourite restaurants and show her my favourite outfits. I want to dress up with her and go on mother-daughter dates. I don't feel like I've ever done that. Why did the four years I had with her have to be the earliest four years of my life? It's gutting really. You always wish you appreciated the time you had with someone when the time is taken away. I wish I had one thing I knew about her, from only me, so I could have some form of soul connection.

I used to write letters to her all the time but I didn't know who I was talking to which made it feel really one-sided. Even visiting the cemetery feels weird to me. I go and I will forever go but I don't know the person I'm going for. There's always this distant feeling that just lurks around all the time and will never go away. There's no ability for me to form a close relationship with my Mum anymore. She knew me but she knew the version of me before I could even be anyone.

Eve MacFarlane

Throughout my late teenage years, I really wanted to connect with my Mum. I wanted to talk to her, to write to her, to pray to her but I never felt the connection. I didn't know the person I was trying to reach. I felt so robbed of my time. I still do. Everyone who knew my Mum knew her better than I did. Even my brothers' old school friends knew my Mum better than me. Even the people who knew her for five minutes at the school gates knew her better than me. Who am I to answer people's questions about her life and who she was? I wanted the mother-daughter connection I'd seen so many times through other people. So desperately. But that will never be possible. I want to have lunch dates with my Mum and be around my Mum and Nana together, but that can never happen and it plays on my mind so much. I wonder so deeply what life would be like with her or what life was like with her. Those four years I had were so miniscule to me because I don't feel like I even lived them. But I can't get them back. Even if someone described to me every second of the time they saw me with my Mum, they wouldn't be able to tell me the time I had with just her and me alone. What about the conversations we had? What did she say to me? How did she deal with my tantrums and how did she spend her time with me? I almost wish I could go back in time and be a spectator to the times we had. Four years is a long time but not when it's a time where you don't have the ability to feel anything. She would have been able to

14 Years Later

remember who I was and what I was like as a toddler but I just don't know who she was.

I was so desperate to discover new things about my Mum's life to build an image of her and understand who she was. I used to ask my Dad countless questions but it was never the same as really knowing her. My proper questions started at a much later age which means her death was distant in the past so it's hard to remember everything. If I asked these questions a year after, maybe I'd know more. I know I could ask lots of people now anything about my Mum and I have done but at this point, it partially feels too far gone. Like I ran out of time. But the time I had, I didn't think to know more.

I came across her diary. It was a 2007 diary and there was a bookmark. The bookmark was open to the week of April 15th. It felt weird. It hadn't changed. The diary was how she left it. Almost as if she was the last person to touch it. When I saw the bookmark on that week it did resonate with me for a while. It was like the only thing I'd had of her that felt like I was the first to come across. I know I wasn't but because it was as if it was untouched and left as it was, it felt like she wasn't so distant from it. Everything she had, over the years, it becomes less and less close to her but this diary felt quite different because of the fact that nothing had changed. I looked through and found dates like 'Sam's parent's evening - 6pm' and

'Eve & Sean's party'. These events were at the time I felt like I never lived. It made it all feel more real again. It was like the proof that she existed so normally before April because as I've said, it feels as if it's made up or all just a story that I've been told. It's weird to think that everything was just so normal when she was around.

I don't remember the places I went with my Mum and the things she said to me but these dates in her diary made such a difference. It was like I found a real part of her, with evidence. A part of her that involved me and my life. I also found her purse. It was just how she left it as well. Almost as if it was still in use, not years and years old. Just laying there untouched. There was a Boots membership card, a Tesco clubcard, a few coins, such normal things to have in a purse but to me, the more I find out about her life and the normalities from her life just makes it all feel stranger and stranger. Like I'm constantly learning more and more about someone that I should know better than most people. A purse and a diary is used pretty much on the daily so casually and so it just all felt so strange and real to me.

A couple of years back, my auntie gave me my Mum's handbag, another item used often by someone. There were lots of her things inside from over the years. There were some cross-stitch pieces she had made and photos with us. More things to help me build up an image of

14 Years Later

who she was. Sometimes it just feels hopeless though because it's like I have all of the materials to form who she was, the stories, the belongings, the photos but I'm just without the most important part, the person. There's such a barrier between the distance and understanding who she was.

Writing has been a big part of my life. I always write. It's a way to express myself and I always have things to say. My Mum's death has always played a huge part in this. It has inspired me a lot to tell my stories and explain my hurt. My brother once told me that our Mum's passing encourages him to succeed in life. I can relate to this. I want to achieve big things. I find strength in the pain I feel. Like I am experiencing this and I will incorporate the pain, anger and passion into my writing. I've always been quite good at expressing myself, whether that's due to speaking to several counsellors or just finding my own methods, I'm not sure but writing just feels like therapy to me. It makes me feel understood and helps me rationalise my feelings. I think I feel things very deeply and so writing helps me find validation in it all. I have written an extremely personal poetry book called 'Dancing In A Crowded Room' which helped me severely through so much and gave me a productive focus. It helped me rationalise my experiences and project my feelings onto something that is my own and that I can be proud of. I am quite a passionate person when I really believe in something and so when I channel that passion into writing, it really does a lot for my mental health. My poetry has aspects of very personal feelings and sadness that I've felt in my life. It also helps me become more familiar with my pain and mentality. It's a good way to find understanding from other people this way. Especially from my Dad. I think it's a useful way to express myself to him more clearly.

I have always been close with my Mum's family. We see them often and have always made great memories with them. They've always played a big part in our lives and made an effort to help with our upbringing as growing up we would always see them and go to different places. Looking back, it does make me think about it all properly and double take. Everybody knew we were growing up without a Mum and they put all of this extra effort into trying to fill that void for us.

Sometimes we'd have family parties and gatherings which have always been fun and a good time to catch up as we don't live near them. I do wish I lived closer to my aunties. There's only so much of a relationship you can build up with people when you don't see them all the time. The family parties have always been happy but sometimes, it does feel like we're that bit separate though as our Mum was the connection and she can never be there. Especially, looking around at everybody

14 Years Later

else having relationships with their Mums and my Mum's sisters. I've tried to visualise who my Mum was based on her siblings and if she was in any way similar. I've always wondered what she'd be like with her family and how she'd act at these family gatherings. I'm sure if she could be there, I wouldn't have even really thought about what she'd be like but you don't really notice these things until it's so definite that you can never experience them again.

I was told my Mum and uncle had a close sibling relationship when they were younger. He recently got married and I wish she was there to see it. I remember being told that she'd be so proud of me as a bridesmaid at that wedding. My auntie also gave a speech mentioning her and it was so emotional. It's times like that, that you really wish she was there to see. I wish she could have seen us all. I wish she could one day get the chance to see me get married.

I notice my friends' Mums are always loving and caring towards me. I connect with them. I guess because they are mothers themselves and would be in the same position as what my Mum would have been in. I always pictured my Mum being friends with my friends' Mums. I think she would have been. It's not as easy for a father to be friends with other Mums. When you're in your late teens, your parents feature less in organising where you go and who you see. They don't need to walk or drive you to places as much anymore and so as you get older, the need for parents obviously fades. It turns more into just wanting them around rather than needing them and as you get older, you begin to understand their care and appreciate them more. I would have loved to buy my Mum flowers often and gone out with her. It's such a shame that it has gone this way. There is and always will be so much I wish I could do.

My Mum's death wasn't so evident to me but the absence she has left has always been obvious and features in my everyday life. The emptiness is so clear here. It's not a hole that can be filled. It's not like losing a toy that you can replace by finding a new one. It is something that is incomparable and will never be fixed. I wish my connection with my Mum was stronger and I wish that I had a memory or something to use to feel close to her. Sometimes, it feels like my only connection to her is our blood. It's weird to me because I know my Mum the same way my friends do. They know what she looks like just as much as I do.

When someone tells me something about my Mum, it literally feels the same as when my Grandpa tells me stories about people from his childhood. That's how distant it feels. Like this woman didn't exist in my

14 Years Later

lifetime. Someone so important to me. The only thing I can really gauge is an idea.

I took some time over the past few months to speak to a lot of family and friends about my Mum's childhood and her life. I always wish I could hear first hand about her younger years like I do from my Dad. Like I could know what she was really like. I've been told about the holidays they went on and the places they all travelled to. My nana used to foster children, even with five of her own. I learnt about all of the houses they lived in and what they used to get up to when they were young. I learnt bits about her adult-hood. I was always told how much she loved being a Mum and how she felt her purpose was being a mother to my brothers and me.

I also learnt a lot about the funeral and what it was like. There's a photo above my mantle piece of my Mum, brothers and me walking into the sea which my Dad took and a lot of my family have it framed in their home. I found out that it was surrounded by white roses at the funeral. Speaking to friends and family about this period of our lives was really eye opening to me as it gave me a whole new perspective to consider. I learnt about the ways my Mum's death affected everybody and more details surrounding the time. It makes it feel a lot less lonely. There were so many people affected but that does mean we could stick together. The conversations I had with people, they all made me feel like they really did want to talk about it. They had never spoken to me or my brothers about this properly. We were too young at the time to hold a detailed important conversation like this and then time goes on and years go by and it's not as evidently present in everyone's life. People don't know if you want to or can talk about it. But it was nice. I needed these conversations. It does bring it all back but I want to feel it. How do you otherwise process a death like this when you've never had any closure?

There are so many differences in the type of loss you feel depending on who they were to you, whether that would be a sister, daughter, mother, cousin, auntie, partner, friend. Even if you've never met someone, you can still feel their loss. I've had several people tell me this. They never knew my Mum but they miss her. They can feel the hole that they left behind and this proves the importance my Mum had. She had a life to live and had so much yet to give.

I think it's so important in life to have a mother and father figure to grow up with and learn from. They can help to rationalise specific things you're going through and help path your future. I never really had a mother figure in my life at all. It's only ever really always been my Dad and my brothers and me. My Dad has had serious girlfriends over time but from the age of around

14 Years Later

ten onwards, in my young years, I never had a mother's guidance. It really makes a huge difference. For me, it's been much more internal. I think it's something that people miss a lot of the time. Especially people I've met recently. The difference in how you live your life isn't always so obvious. So many people don't realise this though. Naturally. It's not easy to fathom. I think people just fail to realise that for me, losing my Mum is very much a personality trait.

Eve MacFarlane

Childhood

Early childhood mostly felt pretty normal to me. I didn't really see myself as separate from everyone else. I simply went about my life as a normal young child. I had loads of friends and I was always busy playing outside. My life just felt normal, though. I hadn't known any different. Growing up without a Mum had always been the way for me so I never really noticed the instant change and shock of it all.

The most I can remember is briefly the downstairs of my Mum's house. The living room and the kitchen. I've walked down the street several times but don't really remember the time I spent there. I had a neighbour across the road who was a little older than me who I used to play with and her Mum still always says hi to me if I bump into her. I roughly remember sections from the inside of her house. Also, I was told we had a swing bench in the garden and I remember having a grey pet rabbit. I don't remember the upstairs of the house or what the garden looked like at all.

My primary school experience was always really enjoyable. I really liked it. It was a very close-knit friendly community school. I had lots of friends, ones who I still speak to. Everything felt pretty normal for as early as I can remember. Although, I went to the After School Club every night until 5pm. I didn't really like being there so late because I just wanted to be at home and play like all of my other friends but it became a part of the routine. I don't remember the days where my Mum picked me up at the gates. I was only in Nursery so I think we only had half days anyway. I remember going to a play-group called Auntie Barbara's. It was a small yellow building but I remember it feeling so much bigger inside. There was a stage at the front and a garden outside with a circular path and pink flowers. I spoke to Barbara over text recently and a couple of years ago and she remembered me so I updated her on how I was.

I vaguely remember several different people giving me lifts to the playgroup and sitting in the back of their car in a baby seat. I'm pretty sure the play group also had little christmas shows as I've seen photos of me dressing up in different outfits. I had a friend called Toby in nursery who's Mum also drove me there.

I was told that shortly after my Mum died, I was taken to get some counselling but apparently I thought I was being taken to go and see my Mum and so when I got there I was asking where she was. What do you say to that? I was also told my behaviour was a bit all over the place after my Mum passed which most probably just stemmed from confusion as I had no idea what had happened to her.

It was only really during my teen years in high school that I started to properly realise and come to terms with the huge gap in my life. I understood that this had disrupted the foundation of our family. I felt like I was missing out on quite a lot. One of the days that this was always extremely apparent was on Mother's day. Everyone seemed to post photos or videos with their Mothers on social media, expressing the friendship and love between them. It is hard to see but it's never not been like that for me. I've become used to it now. I don't feel like I've experienced one Mother's day properly. I can go to the cemetery and visit her but it doesn't bring enough peace to me. It doesn't feel like she's there. To be honest, I don't want to imagine her being there. I'd rather imagine her being everywhere else.

14 Years Later

High school is a place where teenagers are constantly changing and in competition with each other. I didn't really like it. I just found it boring. My high school wasn't known as the best school in the town. When my oldest brother attended it, it was so different. It was much more peaceful and there was a difference in the types of people who were there. By the time I got there, the reputation of the school wasn't particularly the best. This made my year a small year. There were only four forms. My brother's year had ten forms. It was all a bit all over the place in my early years there. It made the experience quite unpleasant. There were lots of dodgy and rough students when I joined which is common for year seven but it lasted until year ten. Most of them had dropped out by then. I enjoyed it sometimes but it was just quite repetitive, as schools usually are. I had lots of friends and spoke to most people in my year a lot but I didn't really like being there. I think I preferred year ten and eleven. I am glad I went though because I met some of the best people there but I do wonder if my education would have been better at another school. Not just because of the education but also how my mental health was during it because I know that impacted my grades. By year eleven, we had a new head teacher who positively impacted the school and made a huge change. It was a shame that it was our last year that he came.

High school was so different to primary school. You become much wiser and familiar with the expectations of life and society. Coming from a house full of boys, it was hard to find anyone at home to relate to and understand me when I was experiencing high school. This was the time where my Mum's death started to dart around in my mind a lot more. I spent a lot of time thinking about it and what life would be like if she was here. During high school, I spoke to a few counsellors about how I felt. It didn't really do much. It wasn't about the grieving that I needed help with, it was about the living without a mother and how easily it was affecting my everyday life. I didn't know how to process it or how to manage a life without a mother. It's not something that comes with instructions or a rule-book. You just have to persevere with it and pray that it all works out okay.

In highschool, pretty much everybody knew about my Mum. I guess people just found out gradually. I was glad because there's nothing worse than someone not knowing and they ask you questions involving your Mum. As normal as it is for me to then say my Mum passed away, it's not a normal and predicted thing to hear. Only five percent of children in the UK are bereaved of a parent before the age of sixteen. Not everyone knows what to say. Most people just assume everyone has two parents. There was one boy in my class whose Dad died when he was six so I can

14 Years Later

understand that he's felt similar feelings to me. We have spoken about it before. It's nice to feel less alone but in the same sense, our situations are still so different to each other so it's hard for us to relate as it also comes down to who you live with and how it's dealt with by people close to you so it could never be the same. We have even spoken recently and it has helped a lot. It's heartbreaking to hear, really. We were such innocent and harmless kids forced to just deal with this life-changing event and we didn't even get the time to know the person. He didn't have any siblings to help him through it all. The recurring question we had was just 'why?'. Why, why, why?

Most of the teachers in my school knew, especially the ones I had quite a few times a week. My maths teacher was really good about it and knew my family quite well as she taught my brother too and was close with my form tutor who also taught my brother. I think she understood it.

Nobody ever wants to ask questions. I guess it's because they wouldn't want to say the wrong thing or upset me. It's a hard thing to approach as it's such a sensitive subject but I've always been okay with talking about it. I guess it's because I never felt the instant upfront shock and trauma that could potentially be brought back with talking. The understanding came so gradually to me over the years, so when something specific is mentioned, I don't feel the instant pain. There have been times when people have mistakenly said something but instantly corrected themselves but this hasn't really affected me. To me, my time with my Mum feels non-existent. The fact that I once had something and now I don't, isn't so visible. I just feel like I've always lived life this way. Sometimes it feels like, how can I miss what I've never had? Maybe it was better like this. I didn't get the time to build up lots of memories or a quality relationship to spend years longing to feel again. The feeling is similar to heartbreak in your life. If you've never created memories or experienced time together, you don't have much to miss so you just miss the concept of having someone there. It's more of the missing the concept of a mother for me.

Something that I struggled to come to terms with over the years was that it could have so easily been completely different. In the sense that, my Mum passed away so randomly. There was no build up and no preparation. It just happened. Through talking to people, I've learnt that apparently the ambulance took forever to arrive and that maybe it would have been so different if it was quicker. You can't get the time back and you can't stop it. I've just never understood what the reason for my Mum's death would be. It's not normal. These things don't happen. I still can't comprehend how simply and

14 Years Later

quickly my life just dramatically changed forever with absolutely no way of turning back time. You're just presented with this life-changing event and forced to accept it.

I've always believed everything happens for a reason in life and that everything you go through builds you up to easily deal with other things. But what would be the reason for this? No reason would be worth it. Taking my Mum away from me before I felt like I even met her?

I wouldn't say I believe in God but I believe in a higher power. I don't believe things just happen in life without reason. I always trust that what I go through in life is to prepare for something else or to stop something from happening. Like if something bad happened one week, it would be to change something worse from happening the following week or month or whenever. For me, I've always believed in my higher power being my Mum. As if she is my guidance and protecting me from things that I'll never know about specifically because she'll keep them away from me. Sometimes when I'm going through something that is really hurting, I trust that I am meant to go through it for valid reasons and that my Mum will guide me out of it. This is just one of my ways of dealing with it, I guess.

A recurring theme that my family told me about when talking to them about my childhood was that when we used to stay with them over the summer holidays, I used to cry so much for my Mum. Like when I'd go to bed, I'd just cry and cry and cry for my Mum's attention. And I could never ever get it. My childhood, of course, lacked maternal attention severely and this was so clear when I'd cry so much. You know when you're young and you have a bad dream and shout for your Mum or Dad, even I used to shout for my Mum as well as my Dad. I knew she was gone but I just thought maybe she could hear me.

I bet my family wanted to cry like I did. I bet seeing me bawling my eyes out begging for my Mum made them so sad. They wanted my Mum too. She was taken from all of us and at that time, it would have hurt them much more than me considering they lost someone who lived through so much of their life with them, especially her siblings. They knew her well and they knew her life. The same with my Dad. My Mum was a physically alive person to them who's life they all saw and experienced first hand.

It's only recently that I've come to terms with the fact that my childhood experience really was extremely distorted due to not being raised with a mother. I didn't realise all of the long-term effects.

14 Years Later

I was told that we were often taken to play centres on Sundays with Mum's friends and I remember always loving places like that. I just don't remember ever going with my Mum. My Grandpa used to take us there a lot over the years which I do remember.

When I was young, I always visualised what life would be like if my Mum was around. I thought about so many things. How I would be living, who my friends would be, if my hobbies and interests would be different, what my mental state would be like. I wondered what places I'd go to, what people I'd meet, what things I'd do, where I'd be right now. It's impossible to know. But it's so strange to me considering my life could have easily been this way. It's so easy to get lost inside these types of thoughts because essentially, it's similar to seeing people's lives on social media and just naturally wishing you had what they had or looked how they looked. It's like a comparison of your life to someone else's. I'm faced with situations on the daily of seeing other mothers and so it's just a constant reminder that to me, I don't have that. Everybody at some point subconsciously compares themselves to others or sees parts of other people's lives that they may be envious of. But who would I be if I had my Mum around?

Eve MacFarlane

During my late teens, I started to think a lot about the parts of a passing that I never really thought about. Considering my Mum and Dad were seperated a couple of years prior, things like planning the funeral, sorting out the financial side, transferring objects and furniture between houses, all of the additional faf that comes with it was more complicated. I don't remember any of this happening. I was too young to be involved anyway, but because I've never really been told about the short-term happenings, it's hard to know everything that was involved. I had two pets at the time. A rabbit called Flopsy and a cat called Paddy. They had to be transferred to a new owner, my Dad, and a new house. I really wanted more pets in my later teens. I feel like I was too young to appreciate them when they were around. I understand that these aspects of a loss are short-term and once they're dealt with, they're dealt with for good, but why on top of everything else, do people have to be faced with these additional elements to sort out as well?

That's the thing about death, it's never straightforward. It comes with so much complication. Even deaths that people may be prepared for. Whether that's just mental complication or materialistic and physical complication, it's not easy.

I've always been fairly close with my Grandpa. I see similarities between him and my Dad and wonder what

14 Years Later

similarities I would have to my Mum. My Grandpa lives in Scotland and so we can only see him several times a year. It's the same with my Mum's parents, my Nana and Papa. With them living in Huddersfield, we don't see them as often as we'd like to. It does make the times we do see them more valuable and memorable though. My Dad has always made an effort to stay in touch with my Mum's side of the family and I have really good relationships with them. I think the two different sides of my family are very different. Just in the sense of having different lifestyles but from what I've been told in recent times, I think my Mum and Dad were quite different too.

The gap between me and my Nana is essentially my Mum. I wonder what similarities they share, what they talk about, how they act around each other. I wish my Mum was here to tell me all about her childhood and upbringing like my Dad can. It interests me. I want to know what it was like from her, herself and how she dealt with certain situations and feelings that she felt. Maybe things I can even relate to. I want her to tell me about her school life and what she loved and hated about it. Her school friends, her teachers, her exams. All of it. It's miraculous how your mind can wander once you know you can't know or have something. Who knew I'd want to know all of this? I know there are people who can tell me as much as they can about her life but it's not the same. I have so many things planned to tell my daughter and places I want to take her. Maybe my Mum had things she wanted to do with me. But we never had the chance.

My Dad tells me about his childhood and has taken me to his schools in Scotland. He's told me stories about his youth and I know the ways in which he was raised. It's just told so naturally but really it shapes who you are so I want to know what shaped my Mum into who she was. In a recent visit to Scotland, I spoke to my Grandpa a lot about his upbringing and his life in the 1930s. It was really interesting to me because he showed me photos from around one hundred years ago. It was like a whole different world. It was crazy to think about all of the different people in the photos and how they all lived their own lives and had a whole life that is just no longer. My Grandpa was raised in such a different society than me. Even my Dad was.

In 1960, 92% of homes had two parent families, now that statistic is 67%. Times are changing. My Dad grew up through a time where single parent homes were rare. Furthering the fact that it wasn't easy for him to know what to do, how to act or feel any less alone in having to raise my and my brothers on his own.

Life nowadays is extremely different to the mid 1900s and there are so many new expectations and priorities. I

14 Years Later

saw a picture of my Grandpa's father. It really resonated with me because this man raised my Grandpa and as a result was such a huge part of his life. The man in the photo looked identical to my Grandpa. Literally exactly the same. It was just so strange to see considering he is my Great Grandfather and how he raised my Grandpa shaped how my Grandpa raised my Dad which shaped how my Dad raised me and my brothers. This also highlights how me and my brothers were influenced to be more similar to my Dad's side of life as we don't have our Mum to influence her way of living. I've only ever known being raised by a man. Not that this is a bad thing but it definitely makes a difference and contributes to shaping your personality as your parents have the biggest effect on you growing up and we never really had a mother's perspective to add to our upbringing. There are lots of factors that influence your personality growing up like who you live with, where you live, what role models you're surrounded with, what friends you have and the places you go. Growing up in a city can be so different to growing up in a town or a village. It can rub off on who you are and how you act. I say this to further my point about how me and my brother's being raised without a maternal figure can affect and change your personality massively. I could be a completely different person if my mother was around.

Eve MacFarlane

After speaking to my Aunties and Uncle, my Mum's siblings, I learnt a lot more about her childhood and how close she was to my Uncle but I still don't have the ability to hear first hand how she herself experienced it. My childhood and how I've been raised could have been so different. Better or worse. It's not something you can ever find the answer to. In so many senses, I am so lucky. I mean, generally, children are raised better with both parents around but the mindset I've developed, I know would not be as nearly as emotionally intelligent as it is now. These are just the types of things I grew up thinking about. Questioning anything and everything. There are just no answers. Bad things happen and the world doesn't stop to let you catch up. It just carries on. No matter how hard you try to make it stop or slow down just for a second. The bottom line is, everyone on this planet is of an equal worth so why would the world take a day off just for you? It feels non-stop. There is no time to breathe in a world where none of my real questions can be answered and I am left with no idea how to navigate my way through it.

Growing up, trying to keep up with the weight and pace of the world without a mother wasn't as easy as maybe I thought it would be. I mean, I know I didn't really have the time to think about how my future would be shaped, I just carried on so naively, for the best. But I always had questions.

14 Years Later

Something I realised over the past few years is that there really are big differences between growing up with a mother and without. They're just not always clear. Even to other people. I guess they wouldn't be to me, thankfully since the life I had with my Mum is hard to recollect. But in recent years, I have noticed how it shapes your personality massively and your view on specific things like your home life, your relationships with friends and people in general, how to act without being able to pick up mannerisms from a mother, I guess it's obvious that you wouldn't realise these things as a young child. It's just a case of it becoming more apparent as you have more experiences. In recent times, through realising this, it has made me understand that the things I've disliked and questioned about my personality are mostly the long-term effects of not having a mother to learn from. I think I just never really realised that when I was younger because I was too young to even discover that there really would have always been long-term effects but to lots of people, my Mum's death is now just a distant memory. But it is still very present in my everyday life. I guess I thought a relationship with a Mum was just the same as with an auntie or a sister. There are similarities, of course, but I've accepted that it's not the same and never will be. However, in areas where there is weakness and loss, there is also experience and power. Everything definitely becomes more clear over time.

Something I've come across dealing with in my late teens is definitely a more unspoken about subject. Maybe a subject that daughters wouldn't even discuss with their mothers, only their friends but sometimes you experience things that you really need to speak to your Mum about. As much education that you get in school and college about safety and contraception and the knowledge that just naturally comes to you as you grow up, it's beneficial to just know that you have a Mum to lean on if anything goes wrong. I'm lucky enough to have amazing people around me who have supported me. I couldn't speak to my Dad about any specific bad experiences. Not because it would be weird or awkward, more so because he hasn't been a girl and wouldn't truly understand it from a female perspective. I have had a really unpleasant experience in this topic and it really threw me off. Luckily, I had people that I could speak to and my friends were really supportive. It also changes your view on men a lot, especially, when you live with only men. You start to feel more uncomfortable. Just in the sense that it is very evident that you are a different gender to the people you live with and it can feel lonely having to pretend you haven't experienced something horrible just because you can't bring yourself to tell them. Over time it changes, though. It becomes a distant

14 Years Later

memory and you feel better and more confident around men. I'm hoping not to over dramatize this either because my experience could have been so much worse. I am very much okay. It actually helped me to speak to one of my guy friends about this. It takes away the fear slightly. It just proved to me that it isn't the specific gender, it's the specific person. There are always some good people around and your judgement of anything can be so tarnished by the different experiences you have had. Women are of course capable of similar actions too but I just don't live with women. The sad fact is, I know quite a few people who have dealt with different forms of sexual assault in their lives. It can range from something so small to something more extreme. Catcalling is even a form of assault but people don't realise this because it has been so normalised in the past. Another title for it is Street Harassment. Two in three girls in the UK have been sexually harassed in a public place and in 2018, 66% of girls aged fourteen to twenty-one said they had experienced unwanted sexual attention or harassment in a public place. Aged fourteen. There is a reason the legal age for consent is sixteen. Catcalling can feel traumatising to someone who has previously been assaulted. It can make you feel like your body is a possession that should constantly be objectified.

Eve MacFarlane

My Dad and brothers haven't really related to this. Some men think it's a compliment but there is a difference between saying something kindly to someone with consideration and shouting wildly at them from across the street. It does change your perception of men, and sex for that matter. I don't live in a misogynistic household in any way, but I do live in a household with people who don't have to fear for their sanity when they leave the house. Me and my friends are catcalled often when we go out but it's just a given now. Why? Because we're so used to it. But sometimes I feel safer with my friends because we're all alert and switched on about it and as a result, dealing with it together. Whereas when you're with men, it's a bit more overlooked. My brother has been good about this in the past when I've explained it and tried to always make me feel safe. But it shouldn't have to be like this. Stop sexualising women's bodies just because they show a bit of skin or may be curvy. It's truly disgusting.

14 Years Later

Dad

My Dad was born in Paisley, Scotland in 1960. He grew up in Glasgow and more recently in his life has visited Gran Canaria, Southwold, London, Frankfurt, Paris, Geneva and lived in Ireland, Glasgow, Berkshire, Bristol, Rossett and Wrexham.

My Dad is someone I will continuously appreciate and always feel in debt of. The strength he had to carry me and my brothers through to adulthood all by himself will forever blow my mind. I'd describe him as considerate, intelligent, trustworthy, reliable and generous.

My relationship with my Dad is forever changing still but we've always been close and spend lots of time together travelling to different places and having plenty of father-daughter days. My Dad makes a lot of time for me and that's what's been useful over the years. It's important, especially, when they become the only parent.

We clash a lot. In the same ways that a teenage daughter usually would with her father but me and my Dad do struggle to understand each other. Sometimes, it feels like we're living in different worlds. Life as a teenage girl is hard for a father to fathom and understand on his own considering he's never been one, himself. Even more so, when he cannot communicate with the mother. I think my teenage life was so different to what his teenage life was once like. Not just because I was a girl but because I was a girl living in the 21st century, not the 70s. It sometimes feels like two different planets and the difference now is quite incomprehensible, especially when social media has drastically changed my generation and is still constantly developing everyday. For someone who never grew up in a time where that was vastly advancing and affecting teenagers' mental health, I can understand that it would be hard to come to terms with. Me and my Dad have learnt a lot about each other and essentially been through a lot together. We know how we can both act and how our miscommunications can affect trying to understand each other. It's hard when you can feel so close to someone, yet at the same time, worlds apart. I've struggled with this a lot growing up, especially in my late teens. I think I just understood that this is the way it was going to be

14 Years Later

but found it hard to accept. I didn't want it to be like this. My friends have always been a huge support to my mental health but I really wanted the help from my Dad. I know it's hard to always know what to say. I get that but sometimes all I wanted was for someone to sit with me to cry to.

It's proven that daughters who have lost their mothers long to feel a strong connection to their fathers. I've always believed this but because my Dad's upbringing compared to mine was so different, and as stated previously, since we feel like we're living in different worlds, it's hard to feel this connection. It's hard to not feel like we're living on two opposite sides of life. We spend a lot of time together and as I've gotten older, I've learnt that the route our relationship has taken was inevitable. I know a lot about how he was raised and what attitudes were present in the 70s. It is so different now. For one, my Dad was raised with two parents in a time where the mother was known to be the primary caregiver. There were countless stereotypes and equality was definitely not as prevalent. It was also during the time that mental illnesses were more stigmatised and not sufficiently spoken about. There was very much a 'just get on with it' attitude. How is he supposed to know how to act and what I needed? And it's not just me. He had two other sons he needed to give his time to.

Eve MacFarlane

It's always felt quite lonely being an only girl living in a house with just boys. The lifestyles feel so different. I've often felt very misunderstood, as if everything is constantly unfair or wrong. Being the youngest, I always felt that my opinions were often disregarded. As if I wasn't any wiser than them because I was too young to know better. A lot comes along with being the youngest child, especially the youngest of three or more siblings. People can be patronising and see you as weak or inferior. But maybe they're the ones inferior because they wouldn't know what growing up without a mother was like if it was right in front of them. It's not a method, it's not a phase, it's not a test, it's not a condition, it's my life. And it's my unwritten and unguided life.

I don't think people realised what it was really like being an only girl with a house full of boys. You build up a lot of strength. I just felt so angry because I was so young and had no real direction or influence on who I wanted to be, especially during late teen years. Watching everyone around you turning into more independent people who rely less on their parents and flip the roles around. I just felt so behind in that because I wanted to be someone who had that mindset. Sometimes I do but it's only really recently. I wanted to be someone that could bring my Mum home flowers or take her out for

14 Years Later

lunch but there never was nor ever will be that opportunity.

I've always felt that women are at a huge disadvantage to men. It's not as safe. Not all men understand this and often disregard it so it can be lonely. Sometimes, I feel like my voice for feminism is drowned out in a house full of men because as I mentioned earlier, my family isn't misogynistic but feminism and sexism isn't as understandable from a male perspective. However, although sexual harassment and abuse can be experienced by men, 97% of women in the UK have reported experiencing this... reported. What about the women that have been too scared to report it? Similarly to this, in ways, I feel like living with 100% men has caused me to have been raised in a masculine way. But really I am the complete opposite. I am into girly things and at a young age, maintaining this girly personality was significantly hard in a man house.

I feel like I'm often seen in the wrong way by my Dad and brothers. Maybe by a lot of people. If you don't know me well, it appears I live a perfect privileged life. I am privileged. I am healthy, I have food, I have a roof over my head. But what does having everything in the world mean to someone who has the huge loss of their mother? Or to someone who often feels spells of deep sadness? Your mentality is less controllable than the materialistic things in life and I believe if it's damaged, it has more of a negative effect. Not everybody will see what's on the inside so it's easy to make assumptions. Money can't buy you happiness. I could be the richest woman in the world but be completely shattered inside. I could have everything I've ever wanted in life and still struggle. I could have all the love from every single person I know but it still wouldn't make up for the loss of love from my mother. I don't have any understanding from my mother either. She's not there to listen to me and respond. I don't know whether it's being a girl without a mother or just being a girl in general that I seek validation and maybe through lack of attention from a mother, it's made me more prone to overthinking and paying attention to detail. I know when your mentality matures, you think differently and your values change but my Mum's loss has definitely defined my mindset and how I think. I've had lots of differentiating opinions with my Dad and brothers. I try to be fair with everything I say and I always believe I am but without the context of my generation, it can come across differently. Growing up in the 21st century is so unpredictable. Even my oldest brother grew up in a society that seems so different to mine. It sometimes feels like I'm surrounded with people in my home who speak a different language but just don't realise it, as if we're all lost in translation somewhere.

14 Years Later

I think a lot about what my relationship would be like with my Mum and if as a girl, it would be easier to connect with her rather than my Dad. I used to be so angry at the world for making this the reality. I've been angry at my Dad for not always being who I needed him to be but he can't exactly be my Mum. There's only so much he can be. I'd look for mother qualities in him, expecting him to play the two parts but it just doesn't work like that. It couldn't work like that. It's been hard to understand that for me because the difference between a mother and a father figure isn't always so obvious. I do wonder if I'm more like my Mum or Dad and what qualities I get from my Mum.

I always dream about the life I want to give my own daughter and everything I'd do and say to her. I have such big ideas. I want to give her everything that I never had. Mentally and physically. It's hard for a Dad to know everything a daughter needs when he has never been one himself. Maybe growing up he just thought he'd only ever have to have an impact on raising sons not daughters, the mother would have a bigger impact on that, right? But not in this case.

Developing into a teenager isn't a simple process normally, let alone without guidance. I couldn't ask my Dad what it was like to have a period and how to cope with it. His guess was as good as mine. I had really good friends in high school who knew this process wouldn't be easy for me. I guess I just kind of got on with it, though. I didn't really understand periods and what to buy or how it worked but neither did the people I lived with. It wasn't a huge issue, though. A few of my friends had started before me and so it wasn't as hard as it could have been.

When people don't know my Dad, they see him as a serious and stern man but he has a very generous heart and would do anything for anyone who needs him. However, I've always felt like he could be angry at the world. I am too. It wasn't fair on him. Because of this, I always believed that my Mum's passing killed a part of him. I mean, I'm sure it did. I'm sure it killed a part of a lot of people but this one is different. How could you forgive the world for stripping you of such an important person in your life?

He is a happy, kind-hearted man who finds joy in lots of things but I've always felt like my Mum's passing silently traumatised him. He's not one to openly express his pain like I do. Anyone would be angry at the world for forcing someone into that position. He has a very prominent 'get on with it' attitude so prioritising raising me and my brothers was his main focus. He wants to see us thrive and create a beautiful life successfully without a mother's guidance. It's almost like he never had a

14 Years Later

chance to really grieve and take time out because there was always so much to do. While going through something like that, your body's reaction is to just go numb. You just have to put a blank face on and act like your world isn't crumbling beneath your feet. It's not real. It didn't happen. It can't be. It won't be. Just pause. Stop. Make time stand still for just a second. Rewind so I can prepare. Take me back to being twenty-one again. Spare me this trauma. Let me wake up in the morning and it all be a horrible nightmare. But it's not a nightmare. You are awake. This is real. And it's happening.

I can't comprehend how my Dad must have felt. It wasn't just grieving an unexpected death, it was realising you now have to change your whole lifestyle and adjust to raising three young children all by yourself. You just silently watch them naively going about their life unable to understand your hurt or even their hurt. They have no idea how this will define and structure their life. You can't even talk to them for support because you're supposed to be their support. We were too young to know what to say or how to act. Do you ever get over the realisation of that reality?

We have spoken about this. Because this is where my pain lies. In the depth of knowing the trauma my Dad felt. But I don't know. I don't feel like I was there. He said to me that having my brothers and me made it easier in ways. It gave him a purpose, it gave him company, it gave him a reason to carry on. But in the same sense, what if you wanted to close that chapter of your life and move on? It's much easier to run away from it than face it head on.

See, I didn't know what it was like to love and lose someone like my Mum. I don't remember the emotional bond we had. We didn't have many years to build it up so I can't speak for anyone who did lose their strong relationship with her. But I can only imagine how it must have felt.

My Nana has always expressed her gratitude and respect to my Dad for his dedication to my brothers and me. She tells him he's doing well whenever we see her. I guess over time, some people who only face the dramatic short-term changes and effects of a passing, it's easier for them to move on from it quicker. You get over grieving but when the hole created is so big and has such a huge impact, it's not something you can just forget about. It still silently stalks you everyday. The loss of our mother is so present and evident in mine and my brothers' lives and it's not something we can just overlook. It really does follow us everywhere.

14 Years Later

I have a close relationship with my brothers. We have always supported each other. We've grown up together as a three without a mother figure. My brothers have been huge role-models to me in life and helped me path my future. I know we all needed each other. Especially through growing up. I can't imagine how everything would be or feel without them. We never predicted our lives to be this way. It's less lonelier knowing I have brothers on this journey with me. I think our close relationship has stemmed from our mother's passing. I've had really deep chats with my older brother about our Mum and what his life was like with her. He knew the day she passed the best out of the three of us. He was nine. It's not a normal thing for my brothers to experience as six and nine year olds. In a split second, someone so important in your life just instantly vanished with absolutely no way to bring them back. I don't know how you come to terms with that. Being so young, it must have felt so confusing and almost not real. I guess they could have felt that it was just a temporary thing and it would all change and go back to normal soon enough. My brother told me he used to have dreams. Dreams about her still being here. I can't comprehend how traumatising it must have been waking up from dreaming. To go from everything being okay to the reality that you are, and forever will be motherless.

Eve MacFarlane

I've never dreamt about my Mum. I think it's because I have no knowledge of her to really dream about. I've never had a dream about having my own Mum either. I guess I just don't really know what it's like and my brain can't feel the concept of it. These dreams would be like a happy escape from reality but you would never want to wake up. Dreaming about having a Mum would only ever be bitter-sweet. I always have dreams and remember a lot of them. Pretty much one from every night which many people are really shocked by actually. Usually this is more during a process where I'm going through something. However, I do remember having several dreams about losing my Dad. It is known to be a common occurrence when a young person's parent dies. This was rare for me but they did sometimes happen in my primary school days. I just remember them really scaring me but I thought, being young, it was normal to dream about that.

14 Years Later

Mental Health

My mental health has been extremely up and down over the years. I have good days and I have bad days, as any person would. I think my mental illnesses have gotten worse, the older I've gotten. I think it's potentially because I've just become more wise and clear with how life works. In recent years, I've discovered so many differences through not having a mother around and the toll it takes on your health. It's hard because people can know about my Mum but to them it's not always a present thought. You take the time to grieve a death but once that's over, to everyone else, everything is back to normal again and life goes on. But my Mum doesn't come back. I think sometimes people forget that this isn't temporary, it lasts forever.

I've had bad anxiety for quite a while. Sometimes, it's easily manageable but sometimes it can be a struggle.

My brother has always been understanding of this which has made such a difference. Anxiety is a hard one to get your head around if you haven't experienced it. It's constantly changing and varying with every situation. Everyone's experiences of it can be so different. I wonder if my Mum would understand it. In my experiences, my friends' mother's have been more understanding of anxiety than their fathers. My anxiety has played a huge part in affecting my life. Sometimes, it is merely present but other times, it consumes everything. Especially with lockdowns lifting again. There's a lot of pressure to go out and be around groups of people. It's a hard one really because I never want it to stop me doing the things I love. It's hard to not overthink with bad anxiety.

If I'm honest, I've felt quite alone a lot of my life. Not because there's nobody there for me but because I can't identify every piece of my hurt specifically and find people to relate to when most of it is the long term effects from losing my Mum. I've never had a mother to turn to or confide in, at times when daughters usually would. I always thought I would have had a best friend relationship with my Mum and part of me really believes she'd understand me and understand the things I was going through. From what I've been told by the people close to her, she was quite a compassionate person. I try to reach her when I'm struggling sometimes. I would just pray to her to make the pain I feel go away. I wanted a Mum to help me through heartbreak. But she was never there. She couldn't be. I wanted a mother's support but I felt like I dealt with it alone. My Dad had never been a heartbroken teenage girl. Neither had my brothers. In the 21st century, I believe it's much harder to be a teenage girl because the pressure and expectations of social media have become extremely toxic and sometimes I really wish I grew up in the 90s.

With all of my friendships, their mother, before their father, has always been the one I'd be the closest with. I have some really good relationships with my friends' Mums but my friends could never have that with mine. My house is very much a man's house. Based on my knowledge from other people's homes, I really feel like you can tell this is a man house. That's not a bad thing but it does make it feel like it's a place I don't belong in as much. As I've grown up, this has become more apparent. I wanted to add joy and happiness into our home through objects or just traditions. I guess it leads to feeling like over the years, I've developed more of a unique personality compared to my Dad and brothers and I'm more associated with what I want in life now. This is why I dream about the life I want to give my daughter.

Eve MacFarlane

I've had times where I've been really sad. Especially in my late teens. I really felt pain to a deep extent. I was diagnosed with depression and anxiety during high school. It wasn't always so obvious where it was coming from but I just remember being so unhappy with my life. It's such a shame because I have so much to be happy about. It's easy to feel invalidated and unappreciative when I do know how lucky I am with the things I do have but materialism isn't important when you're unhappy. Money can't buy my Mum back.

I do think my mental health has gotten worse more recently than in high school but I'm much more familiar with it now and can manage it a lot better. I often felt anxious throughout school. It wasn't exactly always a nice environment. I had really good friends though. I know I was constantly insecure through school and was always comparing myself to everyone else. I couldn't find any way to accept myself for who I was. I never registered compliments. They just went over my head. I understand that this is common for teenage girls to feel insecure or not good enough during high school at times but the process for me lasted quite a while. I know my friends noticed it because I'd always make them delete photos of me if I wasn't happy with them which just made me feel like I was annoying and more of a burden and I'd always overthink everything. I don't know where it all came from really. I think it could have partly been

14 Years Later

through lack of love from female guidance and potentially stemmed from not having a mother around to tell me I was beautiful or make me feel good. When you don't get the attention and affection from a parent, you seek it in other places. I think it has also made me naturally confide in my friends more which is okay but it can sometimes make me feel like I'm becoming a burden to them, especially as you get older. People become more independent and less reliant on their friends and family.

I wanted to feel the mother-daughter love. Even though my friends were there for me, it didn't really change anything. I felt like I was just fending for myself because I'd go home to an only male house with men who weren't battling with the expectations and standards of society for women.

By 2020, I started to love myself again and stopped feeling so insecure. I was really enjoying college and loved the people I was surrounded with. The year started off really well and I just felt so happy and content with everything. I was laughing a lot more and having fun all the time. College gave me the chance to move on from the past and leave all of the insecurity and bad people behind in high school because when I look back, I hate the thought of it all. I hated who I was and how I acted. I hated prom. I used to struggle to look at the photos from that night because I was just so naive to my future and was so unhappy. I felt like I just looked awful. Prom shopping and preparation should be fun and exciting but it was just stressful to me. My Dad couldn't direct me with it all. He didn't know what looked best and what a girl at prom should have, take or what's really included. Prom is supposed to be so exciting and a fun way to celebrate finishing school but if I could go back and make it disappear, I really would.

I don't remember my friends being as insecure as me. I just felt like the odd one out but I don't know why I was so insecure. I just had no guidance on typical teenage girl assets, like hair & makeup, being hygienic, looking after your skin. I think I just disregarded most of it but I guess my insecurity stemmed from the lack of stability in my home life. I've always said I'm glad I have two older brothers rather than two older sisters but that meant I didn't have sisters to lean on, relate to, get advice from, build strong female relationships with or learn from. It was like I was constantly fending for myself.

When lockdown started in 2020, I didn't think too much of it. I thought it would just be a few weeks at home but I didn't know what came with being stuck at home on and off for over a year. I started to struggle with my mental health again in the early summer. There wasn't a chance to go out and distract myself. I went through a

14 Years Later

long confusing time. I was involved with someone I knew for a very long time and my family knew well but probably should have avoided with hindsight. However, I got involved and this took a toll on my mental health because the feelings I resulted in having during and after this experience were really painful and severe. It took up a lot of my day to day life. I had to force myself to get over things that I so desperately wanted to hold on to. This was never something that my Dad understood. I get it, though. It was complicated and wasn't really something I could easily explain when I was so lost in it all. This was a prominent time and experience that made my depression come back at full force again. It's a weird one because it comes and goes in such varying phases. Sometimes, it doesn't feel as apparent but then I'm not distracted anymore and it comes back. My friends were the ones who helped me a lot during this time because they'd seen me like this before and they knew what my mental health was like. They understood some things possibly more than my family because they were also living in a teenage mind and they knew more of the ins and outs about the person involved. During the time this was going on, I thought about my Mum a lot. I was nearly eighteen and started to wonder what she'd think of me and what she'd say to me in this situation. I just wanted to cry to her. I just wanted my Mum but it was so useless to have that recurring thought because she was never there. Sometimes, I feel like with my Dad, there's a huge unbreakable wall in certain topics that just can't be crossed. Some things just couldn't be understood and talked about. I wanted a Mum to cry my heart out to. I sometimes felt uncomfortable and ashamed to go to my Dad and brothers about heartbreak and situations like this. With it being such a complicated one, it always felt so draining and exhausting to explain. I wanted someone to hug me and tell me it was all going to be okay because I truly didn't believe that it would be. I couldn't really see the end of it, to be honest. I spoke to my Mum a lot about this heartbreak and why it had to be so complicated. I prayed to her. I wanted her to change everything. I wanted her to save me from feeling so lonely and lost. I didn't want to sit up crying anymore questioning why things couldn't have just been perfect. It was so clear that I just needed to walk away but I think I just wanted to feel accepted and loved by someone who made me feel like I'd found happiness because it was so lonely at home and I never had the same love from fathers and brothers that you'd have from a boyfriend or mothers and sisters. I guess this led to the fact that it took so long to find the self-respect I needed to leave. The feeling I had around this person was like a freeing feeling. I never wanted to leave it behind because the highs felt so worth it. He just made all my problems seem so small when I was around him but time went on and it became clear that he was hurting me more than he was making me happy. I wouldn't consider myself as

14 Years Later

someone who'd be blind to the red flags and in this instance, I wasn't blinded, I just believed in him so deeply and I wanted him to prove me right and it's so sad looking back because there were so many people around me that could have and wanted to give me the love that I deserved but I just didn't want it from anyone else. It got to a point that it just couldn't be approved or respected anymore by anyone around me. My friends needed me to leave it behind. It was like the world was showing me every sign to leave and since I wasn't listening to them, I was truly forced to leave because I'd hit the very rock bottom of it all. I had to leave for the sake of my survival. It sounds overly dramatic, I know, but I remember the extent of the feelings I felt during this time and my best friend knows too. There was a time where I had vivid dreams every night for a week about this. I remember every single one. I would just wake up and cry because it was never off my mind and I couldn't escape the pain but no one I lived with understood. Sometimes, I felt like the only time I was at peace was when I was asleep because it was the only time I could escape the sadness. The dreams were always happy and about reaching what I always wanted about this situation which made it so much sadder when coming back to reality and waking up. Heartbreak can feel so unhealthy and toxic, especially when you're sitting around the house not doing anything. It was so easy to get absorbed by it because it controlled everything for me. The places

I went, the people I saw, how I viewed myself. It was kind of scary, especially, feeling so alone at home through it all and without having my Mum there, it really accentuated it all. Maybe my mentality wouldn't have been in a place to have the thoughts I had if she was here. Maybe she wouldn't let my mentality get like that. Maybe she would have saved me from it.

From what I've gathered over the years, I really think my Mum and Dad were very different people. Both sides of the family are really different and it does always make me wonder how she would have dealt with any mental illness I was struggling with. I think the emotional side of my brain was similar to hers. This is what I've gathered from the conversations I've had with the people close to her helping me to understand who she was.

This experience in 2020 really made me question a lot. I questioned a lot about my life at home and how having a Mum around may have changed how this experience panned out. Because it was so unexplainable to my Dad and brothers, I needed my Mum so badly. I think there were only two people who really understood what was happening. As lockdown was on and off during this time, it was hard to find distractions and to see the world from a different perspective. I had to force myself to realise that there's so much more to see and to do outside of the house and outside of this tiny bubble that I felt like I was

14 Years Later

living in. It took me a severely long time to understand that this situation would become so small to me in the long-term. Lockdown with depression was like being trapped in a cage with the tiniest opportunities and lack of space to break free and find the happiness I needed. However, going back to college after the lockdowns brought back the good relationships I had and I even created more. I made new really close friends in my second year of college that helped me see the world differently.

The 2021 lockdown made me realise a lot about my home life and how I was living considering I was constantly at home. I started to pay attention to myself a lot more and what my life was like. When you live an unbusy life, it's very easy to get caught up in your own head and often overthink basic things. This has happened to me quite a bit recently, especially since finishing college. It also highlights the long-term effects of losing a Mum as, I can only speak for my life but maybe I would be busier, maybe I would feel more understood by a mother than the people I live with now, maybe I wouldn't have as much of a developed mind. It makes me wonder what my purpose is. When I go to Scotland, part of me feels like one of my purposes is to look after my Grandpa and maintain a close relationship with him. This is something that I love doing anyway. I don't really know how to explain it properly but when I feel like what I'm doing is worthwhile, that is the purpose of it. This book is one of my purposes right now.

During the lockdowns, I felt really sluggish because I wasn't busy or being productive. The lockdowns made me feel like I couldn't be sad about the things I'd be sad about because my life was seen as so privileged. I had a roof over my head, food on the table, a lovely family, so it felt like I wasn't allowed to be sad or that my sadness was invalid in ways but my problems felt so emphasised because of the lockdowns. Everything was highlighted and I had so much time to just sit and think which dug a deeper hole. I've always been a deep thinker but lockdown really accentuated this.

I started to think about my surroundings. The people, the places, my home and over time, how this town has become such a dark place for me. I feel like it is a place where everywhere I go, I have felt some form of sadness. I've lived in Wrexham all my life and this house properly ever since I was four years old so not much has changed. I only ever remember living in this house. The area hasn't really changed or the people around us. All of my childhood memories from home are here and I see them everywhere in my house. I remember being every age in this house and growing up here. I loved my early childhood and never really found faults but I just don't feel like this home is as full of life as it used to be when I

14 Years Later

was younger. I don't find joy here anymore. I always want to be somewhere else. I feel like I have so much baggage here, in this town, as if it's always surrounding me.

My upcoming plans are to move to Manchester and study English and Multimedia Journalism at University. I want to start a new life. Not in the sense of running away but in the sense of moving on from my past. I know I need to do this. I need to go somewhere fresh with new people and start a new chapter of my life. Just to prove that there really is life outside of where I am. Mentally and physically. I have so much love for certain people here and will stay close to the right ones but I always knew this was for the best. I need a space to breathe and change and find myself again. I've always believed in the quote 'you can't heal in the same place that you broke'. Wrexham, to me, has slowly developed into a place where my sadness lies. I don't like it. There is nothing to do here and the town has just become sad for me. Over time, I know this feeling will fade and maybe I'll miss it. It's a shame because this is my home and it always will be but I don't want to be home for a while. I want to come back in a happier mindset with different dreams and different perspectives, knowing new people and new experiences. I know this is the right choice. It's not just that I want to go, I think I really need to go. I've thought about it for a very long time and really considered my options. I don't want to be miles and miles away from my friends, family and the best people in my life but they know I'm not happy here. It is a sad phenomenon but I'm going somewhere new to grow. I know just because I change my surroundings, it doesn't mean that I will instantly heal but I don't want to hold onto the baggage from my past anymore. I want to live in a busy city and experience a new aspect of life. I've never been a person who wanted to stay in one place. Manchester is the next chapter of my life and I'm yet to discover what it will bring but I am really ready for it. I want to learn more about somewhere new and be shown the variety of the world and find new things to make me happy. I felt for a while that there was no life outside of where I'd been. Like everything and everyone I've ever known are the only things I'd ever know but there is life outside of Wrexham for me and I am going to find it. I can't escape my mental illnesses but I can rationalise and change them with the places I go.

A lot of people struggle to understand mental illnesses and they have the mindset that it'll all pass with time. It is true. Nothing lasts forever but it's the situations that pass not so much the trauma or the connection you have to the experiences. Over time, of course, things change and you manage to get over certain bruises from your life but with depression, it follows you. It plants a seed inside of you and grows. Sometimes it weakens but

14 Years Later

sometimes it stands strong. Just because you see someone laughing, it doesn't mean they're no longer depressed. I don't think I've ever gotten over it but you learn to deal with it in a better way. I'm a happy person. I'm always laughing and smiling but that doesn't change the fact that I feel things very deeply. I would say I am emotionally intelligent which isn't always helpful. I've become able to understand people's pain and analyse their words and actions, like a therapist would. In no way am I a therapist but sometimes, I have felt like I have had to be one to myself. I have worried about my mental health before and I know my friends have too but I know myself well enough so that I know how I'll feel with certain situations. My friends have also learnt this too which is so helpful but it's not always a good thing because it stops me doing a lot of things. For example, my anxiety will stop me going to certain places. This was more in my past but it still occurs sometimes. Especially now with lockdown lifting. There's a lot more pressure to go out and be around people.

Mental health is a very complicated subject. It's hard for people to pay enough attention to sometimes because everyone has places to be, things to do, jobs to go to. It's hard to not feel like a burden. It's easy to fall into a routine of not wanting to talk to people and keep it all to yourself. I've always been one to be open to talking about it but of course there have been times where I've just wanted to keep things to myself, especially when it's a common occurrence. It feels like the more common you are openly feeling sad, the less people value it because it gets to a point where people run out of things to say. It all starts to sound like a cliche. With depression, as it's not something that can easily just go away, the way to make it easier is for a person to just demonstrate their support constantly and make it obvious that they care about you. For me, it's never been about what people say to help me, it's more about how they act and how present and consistent they are.

Luckily for me, I've always had such effective friendship support. Certain people really saved me at times. It's easy to fall back into the sadness routine but I had and still have the right people to help me through certain phases I go through. I'm so aware of the people who see the light in me and have never failed to show me consistent support. My friends are extremely supportive and have always expressed the potential they've seen in me over the years. Specific people have learnt the route of my mentality and have always been there for me. I am eternally grateful because without them, I don't know where I'd be.

However, there are some people you out-grow as you get older, especially in the transition from high school to college. I've had people leave my life who I never

14 Years Later

expected to. Even if that is from a sister-like friendship at such a random time. Friendship break-ups can be similar to relationship break-ups. In ways, worse. Friends can break your heart too. Even when it's people that you soon discover were never as beneficial to your life as you once thought. People can really hold you back. The understanding of this is not always instant. It took me a good couple of months to realise that this was always meant to happen and it was for the better. Yeah, it hurt at the time but you find the courage to accept that if people were going to leave, you should always let them, especially the ones that you know will come back once they realise you're done entertaining their drama. I'm much better off now with the right people and feel grateful about being shown what needed to happen. The right people will always stay.

I think something I've struggled with over recent years is that no matter how much someone could hurt you or betray you, some people will just never be sorry. You don't always get the closure you feel like you need. Some people just don't understand what they put you through even though it may be so obvious. You have to just accept the past for what it is and let it all go. That is where you find your freedom.

Being eighteen, I've learnt a lot. In some ways, feeling things deeply at this age has been worse than feeling things deeply at a younger age. I guess because at this age, everything is a bit more clearer and I'm able to understand myself more but at a younger age, maybe it was better to be more naive with my sadness being blurry. At eighteen, you have much more freedom to do what you want. There is no school to be tied down to and you don't have to be surrounded with the wrong people. Being a young teenager, there's less options and everything is limited. You can't just drive away or move out at the flick of your wrist. Being a young teenager is so repetitive with the routine of school and focus of exams. It wasn't as easy to find an escape from feeling sad.

Recently, over this summer, my mental health has been up and down again. It's hard because writing this, I feel like I shouldn't be sad or unhappy with my life when I have so much going for me. I don't know why my mentality is so harsh. I just feel followed everywhere by some sort of concept that just floats behind me wherever I go and whatever I do trying to make the worst out of it all. I have some great experiences and amazing times which make me so happy and makes the concept lag behind a bit but once I'm alone and not busy it's very much apparent again. I have accepted that this is just the type of mentality I have. It is beneficial in lots of ways in the sense of being able to feel wiser to situations or understand people better. I think a lot of people look at

14 Years Later

me and think that I'm a very happy person and always smiling. I do smile and laugh a lot, especially around my friends but it doesn't mean I'm cured. It's like a temporary feeling of being okay. I could have an amazing day with someone and be so much at peace at the time and then come home and the happiness feeling wears off but some people find it so strange that you can go from feeling on top of the world to rock bottom so quickly I truly don't know. I wish I did. I have to force myself out of specific mindsets a lot of the time and try to really train my brain. I do worry about my mental health a lot because sometimes it's scary to me. I know the types of thoughts my brain is capable of having and I just wish it was so different. I wish I could just change it because I do not want to think about things as much as I do when it so easily spirals into a mess.

I think a lot of the time, my Dad felt helpless with my mental health as if he didn't know what to say or do whenever I'd be sad. A teenage mind is a complicated place. It's not an easy thing to understand but growing up, I guess I never really considered this. Men and women both experience different types of feelings. During my high school years, the anxieties and pain I felt was always so different to how my brothers experienced school. The expectations in highschool for girls are so different from expectations for boys. Not necessarily easier or harder, just in the sense that girls experience high school so differently to boys. Everything is different. This means that it's hard for a male to understand the life of a teenage female in high school and vice versa so of course it wasn't easy for my Dad to understand the pressure and standards I faced. Maybe it would have been easier for a mother to understand having been in a more similar position when she was younger. Living in a house full of boys was quite lonely growing up. I didn't really always understand the difference between living with girls and living with boys until my later teens. It feels isolating. It's so sad when you live in a house full of people yet feel like you have no one. There is a huge difference in the feeling of support from family than from friends. I think it's natural to subconsciously seek your family's approval and understanding more than your friends but I had times where I felt the furthest away from my family. Once my older brother moved out, everything changed. I felt a lot more lonely. My younger brother was the most understanding and my oldest brother did the most to mentally help me. Even if that was just to distract me for a few hours. There's a difference between giving up on someone because you don't understand them and accepting that you don't understand but still being there. This was what it was like with my brothers. I didn't feel like anyone truly really understood me at home. The level of understanding would always reach a limit. I think this is why my friends helped me more. They

14 Years Later

understood my hurt over the years which was so lucky but it meant that being away from them felt lonely. As I grew up, I wanted to spend less and less time at home because I just knew I would dwell on the sadness there. If I was out, even with family, I'd have other things to focus on in a new environment which was better than being at home. Of course I don't know how different it would be if my Mum was around but I do always wonder. Maybe I wouldn't feel so sad at home. Maybe she'd have taken away that sadness and replaced it with her understanding and presence.

I think it's quite easy to forget the different experience of life someone without a mother has because it just turns to normality over time. It's now over fourteen years later and I'm surrounded with people who didn't even know me when my Mum was around which means it's always been this way to them. I guess the only impact it really has on my friends is how it impacts my mental health since your parents don't feature as much in your friend's lives as you, yourself do. My friends have only ever known me with just a father but it feels that way for me too. I've never really known what it was like for me to have a mother. Thinking about it, it's such a shitty situation. I don't know why I have to sit and watch everyone around me have great relationships with their mothers while I struggle to have the same relationships with my Dad and brothers.

Eve MacFarlane

Last year, I started up a mental health Instagram account raising awareness and building up a platform to spread my voice. I have recently gained over eleven thousand followers and started up a blog with the same brand name. My brother has helped with this a lot. I use it as a space to channel my emotions from the experiences I've had into something beneficial for myself and other people. I offer advice and support on both the Instagram and the blog and get lots of interaction from followers. It's something I can be constantly working on and that really helps me as well. Instagram is a hard platform to maintain interaction as the algorithm is complicated. I have even made new friends through it which is exciting.

When I struggled or felt alone, I used music as my therapy for the things I went through a lot of the time. I related to songs I'd listen to that expressed the different types of hurt I've felt through my life, especially songs that tell a story because the experiences that artists have felt, they tell their pain through lyrics and put it into words easier to understand.

Faith Hill - There you'll be
Tate McRae - You broke me first
Madison Beer - Emotional bruises
Taylor Swift - This is me trying
Coldplay - Fix you

14 Years Later

Billie Eilish - 8
Jorja Smith - The one
Olivia Roderigo - Drivers license

These songs helped me find validation in the pain I felt in several situations in my life. It was comfortable to know how I felt wasn't a lone feeling and many people go through similar experiences. 'There you'll be', by Faith Hill explains the connection you can have to someone who has passed away. I discovered this song when I was younger and the lyrics really resonated with me. It's a song that makes me feel close to my Mum. The song 'Drivers License', by Olivia Roderigo is pretty much a heartbreak anthem. I think the nature of the song is an emphasis on how painful heartache can be and the song was released at a convenient time for me to understand the lyrics. Billie Eilish's song '8', is probably one of the most therapeutic songs to me. It has a way of capturing a lot of feeling that tells a sad story in a simple and calming rhythm.

Tate McRae and Olivia Roderigo are artists of a similar age to me who write their own songs based on their life and heartbreaks. They have been very inspiring. Madison Beer recently released an album called 'Life Support' which is a truly heartfelt and heart-wrenching album with really authentic and real lyrics. Music has been such a healer for me and I've wanted people to hear these songs that I find validation in and understand it because sometimes lyrics explain things a lot better.

I was told my Mum used to like Katie Melua's songs. I hadn't heard of this singer so I looked her up and listened to her music. I started to listen to her quite a lot, especially the songs, 'Wonderful life' and 'The closest thing to crazy' so now when I listen to these songs, it helps me feel connected to my Mum, like we're both listening. They are both very chilled and calming songs as well which helps.

I think the feelings I felt in my life and the things I've been through have really shaped my personality and changed who I am. It obviously also changes your mentality but for me, even though it has added harsh baggage, it has also made me more emotionally intelligent and encouraged me to understand people and to want to make a difference. Every experience of trauma that you go through in your life pays tribute to how you feel about certain things in the future. However, it can also be beneficial in ways for growth and self-improvement when you overcome it. As well as developing compassion, I am also a much more confident and chatty person now.

Since I have turned eighteen, I do sometimes feel silly to feel the way I feel. Almost as if I should have outgrown

14 Years Later

my sadness by now. Why am I still upset that I can't totally connect with my Dad at this age? Shouldn't I just have accepted it by now and carried on with my life? But turning eighteen doesn't mean it doesn't hurt anymore. If anything, it means more time has gone on to show that this is evidently the reality and I just have to live with it. Mental health is a complicated one. There are so many different aspects to it. I am just eternally grateful for the people I do have in my life and that have always expressed their presence and care. One day I will create the world for myself that I've always wanted. Everything will be okay. Life is never plain sailing and you have to feel the lows in order to feel the highs. It's okay to be lost in life sometimes. I am turning this dramatic trauma in my life into something powerful and artistic. In no way will this experience overall wrongly shape my life and take away what I am capable of. If anything, I will use it to encourage me to reach my goals and aspirations. I've spent so much time in my life doubting myself and silencing everyone's belief in my potential. I hope this book proves to you that I am finally finding myself and understanding what I am capable of.

Eve MacFarlane

14 Years Later

Outro

I am happy. I feel so much joy and excitement in my life. I have so much love to give and so many places I want to go. I've paid lots of attention to everyone who has been there for me and contributed to easing the journey of growing up without a mother. I am so grateful. To all the Mums who have reached out to me and offered their presence over the years, I remember it all and I think about it often. The words people say, the effort people make, the love people give, is always appreciated. This was the life we were given and we have to just work with it. It's okay. Everything always works out okay. I would never have learned half of what I have without this experience. I hope everyone reading this finds comfort in this book and believes that love should be spread much more. Some people are fighting constant battles that you could know nothing about. It's easy to make a huge difference to someone's life just by offering them your support or doing something so small. I am so lucky to have met the specific people that I have in my life. The writing of this book has brought me so much closure and peace. It has helped me to rationalise my thoughts and appreciate everyone's contributions to my life. Speaking to lots of different people throughout the process of my writing really made a difference and helped me understand a lot more about who my Mum was and the impact and importance she had on people's lives. I've also learnt a lot about myself and realised a lot of things. It's not easy to come to terms with any death. It takes time for the hurt to become more bearable. Without experience, there is no room for growth or development. This book has been so beneficial to me. It has been a heavy writing process but one that has brought me so much peace.

14 Years Later

Eve MacFarlane

14 Years Later

Dear Mum,

I'm sorry we never had the chance to really meet. I'm sorry we missed out on the relationship we could have had and I'm sorry you couldn't meet all the people I wanted you to meet. It breaks my heart that you were taken from me before our relationship even started. I hope you heard me that night when I told you everything. I cried so much for you. I hope you heard all the words I've said to you. I hope you aren't upset that you can't be there for me and tell me everything will be okay. I know it will be okay in the end. I will never forgive the world for making this our reality. I wish I knew you and I wish you knew me. I wish we spoke. I wish I heard your voice. I want to do everything with you but the time was stolen from us. The broken pieces will never reform for as long as I live and I will never understand or come to terms with comprehending what happened to you. I don't want you to be a four year chapter of my life from the past that I can't remember. I want you to be my Mum presently. Every day of my life. I don't understand why it had to be you. If you ever pictured seeing the day your daughter turned eighteen, I hope you pictured that I was happy. Because I am happy. I have a great life and am surrounded by great people. I wish you could meet them. I wish you were here to experience my life with me and see everything I've done. We could have gone anywhere together. I hate the barrier of communication between us and I hate that I'm running out of photos. Our time was so limited and our journey was cut so prematurely, before it had even started. How can I sleep knowing that I won't wake up to all of this just being one long bad dream? You were robbed from this world. My heart will never heal from this and will forever feel incomplete without you. The world completely shifted after you died, Mum. I feel your absence every day of my life and I always will. I hope you're proud of Sam and Sean. They made it through so much and have been such an important guidance to me. They were always the light of my life when it felt like I had nothing. Thank you for leaving us in such safe hands. Thank you for choosing my Dad. Thank you for the strength and inspiration you've given me. I hope you always knew the significance you had in this world. Everybody misses you, Mum. Even the people that never got the chance to meet you. Everybody said you lit up every room you were in and were such a bright light to people. I searched for you in so many places so many times but I was led to nothing. This hole in my life will never be filled and I will never forgive the world for taking you so soon. I used to call your name when I was young and was crying my eyes out as if the harder I'd cry, the more likely it would be that you'd come back and save me. I know you knew who was there for me through everything. You watched it all. But I finally made it. I made it to adult-hood after a long eighteen years. Thank you for

14 Years Later

sending me all of the signs to carry on. I will conquer everything in my life for you and I will become everything I've ever dreamed of. I promise to give my daughter everything I've ever wished for and I promise to give her all of the love that you wanted to give me. We will meet again one day, in another life and we can finally have the relationship we always wanted.

Love you forever,
Eve x

Eve MacFarlane

14 Years Later

Questions & Advice

I decided it would be beneficial to speak to several people in a similar situation to me and for them to express in detail how they've felt over the years. These answers are from people who have lost a parent or grown up without a mother or father figure. I compiled together some questions and answers after speaking to them. The names have been changed for anonymity reasons.

How did the loss affect you?

- Sarah, Female (19) Mother died from cancer

'Severely damaging to me. My Mum passed away when I was ten so I was very present during the time and felt like I lost 90% of myself. I wasn't close with my Dad and so I felt an overwhelming feeling of loneliness as he was grieving in his own way alone. It took away a huge part of my childhood.'

- Holly, Female (21) Lack of a Mother figure

'My Mum was never really present in my life. I grew up with my Dad as an only child and seeked a lot of maternal love that I never had. I didn't have too many friends either to learn from or help me feel more understood. Me and my Dad just stuck together and we were really close as I was an only child. I pretty much navigated my path by myself but my Dad was really supportive in the areas he could be.'

- Harvey, Male (16) Father died from cancer

'I was four when my Dad died of cancer. My Mum didn't really deal with the loss very well and I didn't have any siblings to lean on. I had no father figure to learn from and being a boy myself, I really felt like I needed him.'

- Lily, Female (20) Lack of Father figure

'I grew up with my Mum and sister. We were all really close and made sure to stick together. I only knew my Dad when I was really young, around age three. Me and my sister were a huge guidance to each other and did everything together. We don't really have any memory of our Dad but have confided in our Mum's boyfriend of eight years who has treated us like his daughters. Not having a father figure for the early years of our life definitely brought us closer and really affected my Mum as she felt very alone.'

How did you deal with the loss?

- Sarah

'I used to speak to my friends a lot and was always spending time with them and at their houses. Their Mum's were continuously showing me support which made a huge difference. I will never get over it as I remember it all so clearly but it has become easier to accept over time. I also went to therapy for a while which helped me rationalise a lot of how I was feeling.'

- Holly

'Me and my Dad pretty much just stuck together through it all and supported each other so much. It was really just me and him against the world. We did everything together and although I never had the maternal attention and support I needed, my Dad really made a difference in how I felt due to how he treated me. I did struggle through my early teenage years though as there were some things that my Dad couldn't really help me with but I guess I just got on with it. Having a caring and healthy relationship with my Dad made a huge difference.'

- Harvey

'I really struggled growing up. It was a very lonely time but I always tried to distract myself by playing football with my mates or staying busy. My house was a very quiet house with just me and my Mum and so my Dad's presence was really missed. It has definitely gotten easier over time though.'

- Lily

'As I was so young, I didn't have much attachment to my Dad and so his presence wasn't as missed to me. I am so happy with the Father figure I have now and would never change him. He has shown so much support to me and my sister over the years and acted like our real Dad.'

What advice would you give to someone growing up without one of their parents?

- Sarah

'You can find love and support in other people. Although it may seem like it's the most important thing from parents, it is good to consider that there are other people and places to find the care you need. It gets much easier with time. Don't hesitate to reach out to people. People grieve in different ways and so it's hard to feel understood or if you're acting in the right ways but definitely find someone that you trust and can speak to to feel less alone.'

- Holly

'It will get so much easier with time and you'll naturally navigate a lot of it by yourself. You learn a lot through experiences like this. Speak to people when you're struggling. Don't bottle it up. People will expect you to need extra support so don't be worried about coming across wrongly.'

14 Years Later

- Harvey

'Try to stay active and have goals. It's easy to get lost in everything and question why. A lot of boys struggle to speak to people for help but sometimes you just have to bite the bullet and do it. I used to see my Uncle a lot who I became really close with and was like a second father to me.'

- Lily

'Don't hide your feelings. There are people that will understand what you're going through and rather see you happy than struggling. Don't let it affect your self-esteem and confidence and don't lower your standards'

What have you learnt the most from growing up without one of your parents?

- Sarah

'I learnt that traumatic pain is temporary and does get much easier over time. There is so much outside of your bubble and so much to live for that you haven't discovered yet.'

- Holly

'You can find the help you need from other people. Not growing up with a mother figure really taught me a lot about myself and my mentality. I am a strong woman now as you naturally instinctively learn things on the way.'

- Harvey

'It's good to stick together and confide in people. Growing up without a father figure does obviously affect your childhood and how you are raised but there is so much more to your life than just your childhood.'

- Lily

'For me, the loss of my real Dad was pretty much replaced by my Mum's boyfriend and so his position was pretty much filled. It does make you question a lot about yourself and why he left but over time you get over it and prefer to confide in the people who are morally correct and wish to stay. I have learnt a lot about other people's mentalities and their actions as well due to this.'

14 Years Later

Eve MacFarlane

14 Years Later

Mental Health Information

Depression -
Depression is a constant feeling of sadness and low mood which can last for months affecting your daily life.

Symptoms of depression:
- Loss of interest in doing things they usually enjoy
- Seem to be feeling down or hopeless
- Having less speech and movements
- More fidgety and restless than usual
- Feeling tired or not having much energy
- Overeating or loss of appetite
- Sleeping more than usual or not sleeping at all
- Having trouble concentrating on everyday things such as watching TV or reading the paper

How to help someone that feels depressed:
- Show that you care and can listen
- Gentle encourage them to help themselves, for example, by staying physically active, maintaining a balanced diet and doing things they enjoy
- Offer your time and understanding
- Familiarise them with the services available to them, for example, depression support groups

- Stay in touch with them, by texts or phone calls, meeting to socialise
- Be patient
- Keep them talking

Anxiety -

Anxiety is an emotion characterized by feelings of tension and worried thoughts. People with anxiety disorders usually have recurring intrusive thoughts or concerns and may lead to avoiding certain situations out of worry.

Symptoms of anxiety:
- Uncontrollable over thinking
- Difficulties concentrating
- Racing thoughts
- Feelings of dread and panic
- Heightened alertness
- Problems with sleep
- Changes in appetite
- Wanting to escape the situation you are in
- Dissociation

How to help someone during a panic attack:
- Stay with the person and keep calm
- Don't make assumptions about what the person needs, ask them
- Speak to the person in short simple sentences

- Keep yourself present and be supportive

Ocd -

Obsessive-compulsive disorder has two main parts: obsessions and compulsions. Obsessions are unwelcome thoughts, images, urges, worries or doubts that repeatedly appear in your mind. Compulsions are repetitive activities that you do to reduce the anxiety caused by the obsession.

How to help someone with OCD:
- Be open with them about their OCD
- Be patient
- Don't judge
- Research and find out as much as you can
- Show emotional support
- Be there and listen

Bipolar -

Bipolar disorder is a mental illness marked by extreme shifts in mood. Symptoms can include an extremely elevated mood called mania. They can also include episodes of depression.

Treatment for bipolar:
- Cognitive behavioral therapy
- Psychoeducation
- Interpersonal and social rhythm therapy
- Keep a routine for eating and sleeping
- learn to recognize mood swings
- Ask a friend or relative to support your treatment plans

- Talk to a doctor or licensed healthcare provider

Eating disorder -

An eating disorder is a mental health condition where you use the control of food to cope with feelings or other situations. Unhealthy eating behaviour may include eating too much or too little or worrying about your body weight or body shape.

How to help someone with an eating disorder:
- Stay calm
- Don't judge them
- Avoid talking to them about their appearance
- Focus on how they're feeling
- Avoid discussing people's diet or weight problems
- Do not be upset by their secrecy, this isn't a reflection on you, it's part of the illness
- Try using sentences starting with 'I' instead of 'you' like 'I'm worried because you do not seem happy'

Dissociative disorder -

Dissociative disorders are a group of conditions where you may feel disconnected from yourself and the world around you. Symptoms of a dissociative disorder include seizures, loss of sensation, memory loss and identity issues.

Symptoms of dissociative disorder:
- Feeling disconnected from yourself

14 Years Later

- Forgetting about certain time periods, events and personal information
- Feeling uncertain about who you are
- Feeling little or no physical pain
- Having multiple or distinct personalities

How to help someone with dissociative disorder:
- Stay calm during switches
- Learn how to recognise and avoid triggers
- Take care of yourself too
- Let them know you care about them
- Offer to help look for providers
- Choose a time where you're both free and relaxed to talk

Websites for information on mental health:
Mind.org.uk
Rethink.org
Mentalhealth.org.uk
Ocdaction.org.uk
Anxietyuk.org.uk
Bipolaruk.org
Therecoveryvillage.com

The Samaritans HelpLine - 116 123

Eve MacFarlane

14 Years Later

Thank you, Dad

Thank you, Sam, Sean

Thank you, Charlie, Lia, Doua, Cleo

Eve MacFarlane

14 Years Later

A special thanks to Jacqueline and Steve Taylor, Brian Armstrong and Angela Butterworth, Hazel Taylor and Andrew Taylor, Angela Edwards, Rob Welch, Hannah Welch, Sharon Baldwin, Maureen Allmand, Rachel and Heather Taylor, Karina Pittoors, Sabina Edwards, Kirsty Shepherdson, Sheila MacFarlane, John Newlands, Jean and Walter Armstrong, Dugald MacFarlane, Laura Jones, Soo Moulton - Wilde, Jane Nicholls, Chris McMahon, Carol Burwood and many other friends and family for their invaluable support throughout my life and inspiration for this book.

Eve MacFarlane

14 Years Later

Eve MacFarlane